"To all the young dreamers and artists, May your imagination soar as high as the sky and your creativity know no bounds. This book is dedicated to you, the bright stars of tomorrow, as you fill its pages with colors, shapes, and endless possibilities. Keep drawing, keep exploring, and never stop believing in the magic of your own creations. With love and endless encouragement,"

Luno Prudente

2023

This Book Belongs to:

____

Test Color Page